Part 1: Stunted Growth

An Excerpt from a Book I Cannot Write

He was beautiful in a kind of quiet way; a way in which it was
not obnoxious in the slightest. He seemed to live his life surrounded
by an aura of soft, but electric, energy; something that him inviting
and comforting, wild and adventurous all at once. He himself was an
adventure and a home. Before him, I didn't that a person could be that
- something so safe yet so intense all at once. But he, he was
something else. He almost wasn't even human. And at the end, the
tragic and, what some would call poetic, end, I realized he wasn't. He
was a monster; a horrible and wretched excuse for a person.

It was hot. It was scalding hot when I met him; all dressed down
and masquerading the old cliche of a cool drink of water. He was
refreshing and new, and quenched a thirst that I hadn't previously
realized I had. I was at a concert - what concert doesn't really
matter. I've always been all about detail over big picture.
Regardless, I was with my best friend at the time. We met up with her
best friend. And with her, came him - her best friend.

He was quiet. He didn't necessarily draw all attention to him; he
wasn't jaw-dropping, and when he walked into a room, nobody stopped to
stare. But I did. I don't know what it was, but he drew me in almost
instantly. He was quiet and sarcastic and a little mean, but it worked
for him. When he kind of smiled and said hi with an almost cruel
politeness, I nearly melted. Maybe it was the heat, but I was
awestruck and convinced it was him that had me verging on heatstroke,
not Ohio's ruthless summer.

I was more or less onto him.

Ether

Take me somewhere
and bury me alive
with the dreams I've left unfollowed.
Take me there
and suffocate me
with every word I've ever swallowed.
Don't tell me that I matter
when I'm a compilation of
borrowed memories
and poems already written.
Maybe we can dive into oblivion,
free fall forever,
because there's no way to fix the broken.
Take me there,
there,
somewhere.

          Solemn Do We Fall
                    And Other Lies that Hedonists Tell

You kissed me,
and I felt
that drugless high
intensify.

If I'd have known
the meaning of
Addiction,
I would have
stopped you.

(The second stanza
is a lie.)

Heatstroke in the Height of January

Shallow smiles and hidden intentions,
too much trust and too many confessions.
The day was too hot
and the temperature ice cold.
I fought more than hypothermia.

Confessions of a Storm

Dizzy whirlwind of shakiness,
you either live or you confess.

Memories of Marine Mutilation

Drowning hopelessly in the hours,
unable to think,
let alone escape
the harsh existence
of fate.

                              White Lies

My mind begged for help,
but you never kiss and tell
the truth.

Damned, Consumed, Extinguished

With gasoline tears
and lighter fluid in my veins,
you can strike your match
and I'll let it mean everything
(or maybe nothing at all.)
Your lies are explosive,
and I guess mine are the same,
because two can keep a secret
if they both go up in flames.
(Will you burn with me?)

The Learned Amnesiac's Salvation

So douse me in sweet sedation,
drown me in faux elation,
This is my liberation;
my counteractive salvation.

Because you learn to forget
or you do it again.

Prayer of a Desperate Atheist

And you're at it once again,
you've trapped me in my head,
and if only death will part us,
then please, god, strike me dead.

Delayed Apologies
(To My Abuser)

And I'm sorry I'm still a wreck,
I'm sorry I can't get over this,
and I'm sorry that you'll forget.
And I'd be sorry I'm gone,
if only it mattered.

Warm Welcomes

And now you've returned
when I'm at my worst,
prettier than ever;
rose engulfed by thorns.
I'd be lying if I said
I wasn't begging you for more.

Of course I know
this is what you do -
it's what you've always done -
but I'm too much like I was
to convince myself to run.

Selective Impressions

And I hate myself for it,
but you could continue abusing me endlessly,
and I would keep ripping myself apart
just to find a way
to keep you looking like a god.

Secondhand Smoke

And I think about how
maybe,
just maybe,
everyone is right;
maybe I do this to myself.
He used to burn me with cigarettes,
and now I only date people who smoke.

Part 2: Of Symptoms & Symphonies

Lies, Love, and Other Complicated Concepts

When people ask me how I recovered,
I never know how to admit that I haven't.
I don't know how to tell people who think they love me
that the only reason they're able to love me
is because I start every morning with a concoction of medications
and lock myself in my room when symptoms surface.
I don't know how to confess
that the only reason they love me
is because I've been lying.
All smiles and apologies and downplaying my bad days;
Promising that all the scars are years old and
that I haven't even contemplated ending it
since the last time I attempted
which was, of course, forever ago.
How do I talk to people about the abuse
without telling them that it's my fault I'm the victim?
How do I explain that being the victim is my safe zone?

I guess this is a good start.

Heart of Francium

My heart
hyper, dizzy, manic.
My heart
that doesn't know safe,
that is a stranger to stoicism.
My heart and I,
we have an interesting relationship.
She taught me to be a masochist,
and in turn I stopped trying to protect her.
She doesn't like or dislike or anything;
she loves or hates everything
with a passion much greater
than an entire being should feel
in a lifetime,
much less
one heart
each second of every day.
Under my heart's guidance,
I have fallen
deeply, madly, infuriatingly
in love with everybody
that I have ever been with
(or touched or kissed or seen).
I give pieces of her out
With each step I take.
I am composed of
all-consuming compassion
and hatred hotter than hellfire.
I don't know tepid, mild, neutral;
can't comprehend a normal dosage of,
well,
anything,
really.

                    I am Become Passion

I'm sure that somewhere -
deep down inside -
I want to be stable.
Something in me must be fighting;
clawing, biting, screaming
for the right to be neutral,
But I do not know this part of me,
not personally.
Because,
the thing is,
every piece of me is
Clawing, biting, screaming;
caressing, kissing, singing.
I don't know neutrality;
this ideal of being
perfectly,
imperceptibly
stable -
it scares me.
My mind, body, soul,
we do not know how
to be
quiet
without feeling physically silenced
or to be
vocal
without the presence of a metaphorical soapbox.
We don't know how to kiss
without handing out pieces of us;
or to cry
without drowning a continent in oceanic layers.
We are not an ocean on a mild and temperate day
but an ocean in the midst of a hurricane;
not a forest in the spring,
but a forest ablaze with a wild fire of its own creation.
We
or I,
or whomever this fiery ocean of feelings belongs to,
do not belong in Minnesota or Nebraska,
but southern africa in the middle of august;
Antarctica in the height of december.
Oppenheimer may have become death
upon the day he created the nuclear bomb;

but I am become passion,
the day I came into this world
and every day onward,
as I continuously seal my
nonexistent fate;
made up of manic choices
and
near death experiences.

Artful Asphyxiation

I wish I knew how to
relate to beauty, life, wonder, joy,
but my strife is holding a knife
to my neck,
and honestly I'm in love with
the sensation
of having difficulty breathing.

                              No, Never

I've fallen into this odd habit.
I write all over myself
signifying what I think or
symbolizing who I really am
or whatever the case is.
A planet on my thigh in metallic;
I don't think I belong here.
The word "pretty" on my stomach in felt tip;
maybe, some day.
"Run away with me" on my wrist in multicolor;
perhaps I'm in love and
perhaps neither of us belong here.
Lines everywhere in broken glass;
where is here?
More incisions in reflective metal;
maybe means no.
Uneven patchwork on my neck in fingernails;
here is never.

Words Lose Their Meaning

I think it really it me,
~~what you had done to me~~
what I had done to myself
when you told me you'd never leave.
Because those are weighty words but,
to me,
they mean absolutely nothing.
At this point,
I didn't care who stayed and who went.
You either stayed long enough for me to push you away,
or you left when you realized I'm not a manic dream, after all.
Either way, you would destroy me.
Either way, it was my fault.
Either way, it didn't fucking matter.
Did it?

All My Deadly Desires

Maybe I have a fascination with death.
I've always leaned toward suicidal thought and tendencies,
and I've had a plethora of diagnoses added to the list for as long as
I can remember.
But it's deeper than that;
it's not just a chemical imbalance
or something a pill or 9 can fix.
See, it's the people I surround myself with,
my obsessions,
my love of vices.
I dated a guy who smoked a pack a day
(I started smoking.)
I dated a girl who took long walks at night with no form of
protection.
She lived across the country, I couldn't walk with her.
So I started walking alone, too.
(I left my knife and mace and phone at home.)
I dated a boy who obsessed over body image.
He didn't eat much, so I stopped eating altogether.
(I wanted to be small enough for him.)
I dated a guy who shamelessly encouraged my self harm habit.
(I ended up passed out on his floor.)
I'm seeing a girl who texts and drives now
I don't drive, but I'm sure I can get creative.
(I don't know how to not be destructive.)

Near Death Experiences

It is nights like these between branches like barbed wire
that I crave something malevolent, or maybe unholy.
When my veins pump something acidic to my heart, which
beats as if it's in a horror movie but - this is to say it rests.
I, however, am restless and need something, anything, that goes up;
up toward the glide of bats in hazy moonlight.
This is a place of strangers -
strangers and nostalgia and something darker.
Mania, maybe, waiting for an inappropriate time to introduce herself.
She whispers sickly sweet ideas that quickly turn bitter when they
prick my skin.
I shiver, but only at my own wicked desires,
or maybe sins of my past lives or eighteen years,
and maybe I wonder about the hell that I don't really believe in,
but do sometimes, when things are bad.
But up in the atmosphere with my mind on the opposite of paradise,
if such a thing exists -
paradise, that is -
I am thinking of anything but death.
I feel alive and like I'm evolving - no, transcending - something
absolute.
We get drunk on flower petals and something that burns,
high on blood and something that can't quite and never will be god.
They tell us to come down and we can't or won't,
but either way we follow our instincts and look the grim reaper in the
eye.
It isn't our time but he demands to know who creeps out of graveyards
each night,
shrouded in fog and cloaked in ambiguity to mock his failures.
Humanity has a body count higher than your god,
and doesn't that make you wonder?
Lie me on the alter of a lie of your choice and slice me open.
Watch as my blood pools out, and ponder on how it doesn't matter,
really.
Touch my swollen lips and ask what you did to extinguish the eternal
fire.
Hide my body when I don't answer and search the sky for lightning or
new constellations or the aurora borealis.
Shrug it off when all you see is black.
It is time that you reflect on all that you have and have not done;
all that you have considered genuinely and all that was fleeting.
What is magic, anyway? Or, rather, what is being alive -

no, what is dying and who are we?
What is blasphemy if not the most basic principle of humanity?
And what does it matter, really, that we made it all up?

I Record My Therapy Sessions

I have trust issues.
I've always been rather paranoid, sure,
but I guess a lot has gone into it over time.
Once,
in therapy,
I was so manic,
I was rushing and slurring and stumbling over my words.
My therapist was furiously taking notes,
and I became overwhelmed
with the idea that he was faking it,
that he had given up on me,
that he wasn't listening to me,
that he was just scribbling at random.
I grabbed his legal pad,
suddenly hysterical,
ready to prove my fear.
Naturally, I was wrong.
He's a professional,
and I'm nothing special,
and now I'm too ashamed to voice my doubts.

White Flag

I quit therapy again.
At the time,
I was under the spell
of independence.
I realize now
I traded in my safety net
for endless sleepless nights
full of impulsivity and faux elation,
followed by
endless drowsy days
filled with nothing but a numb sadness.
Maybe I don't want to get better.
Maybe I stopped believing I can.
I'm scared it doesn't make a difference.

Run Away with Me

Fly straight til morning
after you hit the second star,
and then maybe you and I
can learn to patch our scars.
We can talk about the days
when our hopes went unharmed,
and maybe this time
we'll make it a little farther.

The Skeptic's Experiment

I Fell to my knees at 11:11
and prayed to a fucking star.
I knew that it was pointless,
I'm just so goddamn fond of scars.
And so
I tossed my life into a fountain
in exchange for a wish,
it ricocheted off the porcelain
and I knew that I had missed.

Body Like a Prison, Mind All Rage and Shriek

Darkness trickles down my throat like sickly sweet ambrosia;
I am a fallen god and I refuse to cough the poison up.
There is a weakness in feigning an angelic soul,
a strength in acting on the wickedness that taints.
The corrupted fantasies that swell within
are the truest reflection of real intention,
and I am all blossoming bruises and teeth ripping innocence from the
source.
The power of christ compels - no, repel
the rebel angels or holy demons that creep from depths to forefront
and you hold the key to the breeding of eternal misery.
A coin is two sided and so are you,
trying so hard to be above the crowd of crime and craze
but you are one of the animals
and it's time to embrace,
no,
redefine your destiny, fate, life, self.
They say take a walk on the wild side,
but the only way to taste blood the way the Greeks did
is to nose dive from steep cliff to shallow stream
and come face to face with your own mortality.
Go to church and you're kidding yourself,
lose control and you go to jail,
but what's the difference when they've all got the same principles,
anyway?
STop suppressing the internal conflict and bring it to reality,
by reality I mean external, explicit, expel.
If you want to be real you've got to get your hands dirty,
and quite frankly,
smoking a cigarette in secrecy and knocking back a tequila shot is far
too tame.
Thrust your claws through flesh and ribcage to feel beating, bloody,
basic life being reduced to pumping organ
and death of creation to nothing more than a sick and primal thrill.
You want to be okay?
Stop lying to yourself and let it all out.
The chaos and echoes of lost desires.
You're no angel nor devil, no hero or villain.
Life's too storybook and you have the pen.
You want control?
You better learn to lose it
or you'll be nothing but human,
barred behind what you think you're supposed to be.

You want reality?
You better bleed it out of your pretty veins
or you'll be dead long before your heart stops.

Pros and Cons of Invisibility

But pain is only understood
when it is outward,
and so my mind
meaning nothing to you,
and I find
that I am fine
with that.

The Lament of the Struggling Writer

Poetry;
everything to my soul
and better than oxygen.
Though, I should note,
twice as deadly.
Reality;
sometimes
things are exactly what they seem,
but don't try to tell me that.
The poet;
always a slave to metaphor.
The realist;
I wouldn't know.
Would you?

Little Lies Meet the Ugly Truth

When it comes down to it,
there's nothing poetic about this life;
nothing inherently poetic about being a poet,
about being mentally ill due to
flawed brain chemicals
and worse experiences.
Really,
it's choking down uncoated pills,
chalky and poisonous on my tongue,
gagging
so I'm easier for everyone else to swallow.
Washing down my prescribed death sentence with cheap wine,
because it's less depressing than vodka, right?
It's not alcoholism if you drink out of a glass
(no matter how many times you fill it.)
You write poetry on a crumpled napkin,
hands shaking response to your chemical reaction.
You want desperately to explain the world
via pretty prose and half-assed verses,
but really, it's not poetic.
Really, it's a glorified death wish.
Really, they're the same thing.

Counterintuitive Solutions

I'll destroy my veins just to remind myself
that I am a living, breathing vessel
home to a galactic soul,
that has yet to find its home
in this polluted expanse of space.

And I'll refuse my pleas for basic needs
all to watch myself whiter away.
The absence of satisfaction
is what reminds me that I am real,
and that one day
I will die.

Story of an Anonymous Artist

Oh, what a place to be
inside an artist's mind;
chaos and ghostly memories
create such magical things.
Relax and stay awhile
and maybe waste your pain
on 3 a.m. projects
that no one will ever see you;
save a split nail here
or pain in your hair.
You're cordially invited
to destroy yourself
and create something more;
something permanent
that's believed to be worth it.
Because, after a while,
artists do not just create their work,
they become their work.
And so immortality is not too far off
in a way
but it depends on your mindset.
And this is where artists divide;
for you either dream of never dying
or you have a countdown.
Oh, what a beautiful thing is is to disagree.

Sugar Crash

This is the aftermath.
This is the part where I realize I broke all of my good habits.
This is the part where everything hurts.
This is the dehydration and twitching and shaking -
shaking, so much fucking shaking.
I used to think I couldn't still but now I'd give anything for still.
It's fun when you feel like you're flying but less so when your eyes
are rolling back in your head.
You know, when you're alone.
Or when you feel alone.
It's the same, really, isn't it?
This is realizing you let your genetics and your manic depressive
desires consume you.
This is when your friends tell you you're being dramatic.
They've done worse - what am I scared of?
What am I afraid of?
I'm fine.

I Was Running Away, but I Couldn't Tell You What From

Do you ever look in the mirror for answers?
I don't lie on the whole, but that doesn't keep me from fooling
myself.
I don't tell lies, but I don't think that makes this shit the truth by
default.
Sometimes, when I don't sleep, I think I'm that much closer to
honesty.
Something about the way the moon settles in the sky
behind thick winter clouds and vicious Ohio winds -
the way it glows through anyway and the way I wish so badly I could
taste the light.
I wish so badly I could have the light,
but I lost the life I held so carelessly years ago.
And what is life if not light?
And what am I, if not the absence of?
I can tell you I'm all spilled blood and blackened lungs
and flesh that can never feel the sun.
Sometimes I feel subhuman,
and sometimes I feel as if the very essence of human nature
is feeling less than.
Sometimes, I get so high, I begin to imagine wind storms.
Sometimes, I get so high, I can almost pretend I don't exist.
Do you ever get the feeling you're not really awake?
Me too, but I also don't think I've ever really slept.
I am all chaos and dehydrated veins;
internal bleeding and fist sized bruises.
Maybe I am the storm.
Maybe I'm god -
but what's an immortal that bleeds?

Incomplete Identity

I exist most purely and truthfully
in the most fleeting of my gestures.
I think strangers know me better
than my best friends ever could.

Funeral Hymn

I'm most easily described as a graveyard.
Restless spirits gliding through my veins,
ghostly teenagers getting drunk on my pain.
It's insane
how romantic I make suffering look, they say.
But they never take a moment to pray
for their favorite mesmerizing decay
and its deadly allure.
Are you sure
you don't want to spend the night?
Why can't you look at me in the daylight?
Why are you most in love with my shadows
and the bruised skin beneath my eyes?
Why do you call my manic stages sexy
and my suicide attempts beautifully arresting?
I know I should be used to people
walking all over my headstone
and the anger people feel
when my spiritual deaths aren't lovely anymore;
aren't just another broken score.
When I don't wake up
and shatter the manic dream
turned depressive nightmare.
Baby don't stare
at my scars like that -
the sun is out
and you need to go home.

Part 3: Yellow Bird Illusion

The Moment I Fell in Love with a Professional Liar

I don't like to be touched. Touch is . . . violation, invasion,
decimation. Touch is stripping me of what is mine, what has taken me
years to reclaim. Touch is taking advantage, touch is using, touch is
the absence of love. Touch is dehumanizing, dangerous, deadly. Touch
induces fear. Touch hurts, wounds, scars.

And you, you don't "touch" me. You caress, explore, feel. It is raw
and hungry, intimate and lovely. Natural ebb and flow from soft and
sweet, to urgent passion. You consume me, but it's okay, because I
want you to. I never got that chance with him.

First Wave

September 9th, 2016

You say you needed time,
you just wanted something more than this.
I was hopelessly missing you
while you were staring at her lips.
Now you say I'm what you want,
but I'm terrified to rely on that,
because next time we hit a rough patch
maybe you'll go through with Kat.
I love you and won't leave,
please keep wanting me.

September 16th, 2016

You didn't.

Question Everything

Months of beauty, shattered;
real desires, revealed.
He needed a week to realize,
now you'll need years to heal.
Write to process the pain:
he doesn't want you anymore.
Carve it into your skin if you have to,
what else could he have been aiming for?
Now he plays the prince,
claiming it's what's best for you.
But do you think he cares?
Does he even think of you?
He doesn't want you anymore;
hollow love with lack of desire.
He doesn't want you anymore;
stifling the once eternal fire.
Ask yourself: did he ever?

                                    3 Minutes

8:56 on a Tuesday night,
everything I'm supposed to do
a chaotic jumble next to me
untouched, because I'm thinking of you.
Why?
Why do I do this?
It's raining.
8:59 now;
could've sworn it'd been hours,
but I could've sworn you loved me.
My perceptions,
always skewed.

Treat Others How they Deserve to be Treated

He said, "I feel guilty whenever I think of you."
I thought, against my desperate desire to be the bigger person,
Good.
I want you to feel every last drop of what you did to me
without so much as a second thought.

Snapshots

Do you remember our first date?
I remember snapshots.
You walked up to my house in jeans and a Rolling Stones shirt.
I saw it as a sign; I was named after one of their songs.
Perhaps I should have taken into account that it's a breakup song.
As we started our walk,
you asked me if you "should" hold my hand.
I remember not wanting to answer, fearing that you didn't want to.
I wonder if our relationship was like that;
did you want it, or did you just feel like it should have happened?
We ventured onto private property -
the trees looked pretty at night -
and you said you didn't think I'd do something like that.
Maybe, if you had altered your perception of me right then and there,
things would have been different
(they wouldn't).
I took you to my favorite park.
We watched the stars, and you asked if I would let you kiss me.
I blushed and said nothing;
you kissed me, and the night became real;
real and alive with magic and maybes.
We ended up caught in the rain and found shelter under the awning of
my old elementary school.
You leaned me against the bricks and kissed me again,
a little more passionately this time.
You didn't say anything, but your lips told me that you had been
waiting for this;
that kiss made me feel wanted.
We then found ourselves sitting on the steps of the memorial.
We talked and you took a picture of us,
and then you asked me what I thought would happen with us.
I didn't say anything, again, too insecure to say anything of
substance.
You kissed me again, and asked if that helped me answer.
I told you I liked spending time with you,
that something about it felt right.
I wish I kept my mouth shut,
or maybe I just wish I lied, instead.
Finally, we made it back to my house.
You asked to see my room, and I brought you in.
My mom was asleep on the couch.
You asked me to put a record on;
I chose I'm Wide Awake It's Morning by Bright Eyes,

a personal favorite of mine.
You kissed me to it,
and that's when you became my yellow bird.
When you kissed her,
the idea of a yellow bird became an illusion.

Do you remember our first date?
I remember it better than I'd like to.

                    In Case You Were Wondering, I Didn't Forget

We were,
in concept,
a lovely,
beautiful,
magical cliche.
The writer
and the musician;
you could compose
symphonies in my rib cage,
as I wrote stories for your lungs.
But,
we were,
in reality,
a tragedy;
passion burned bright, but,
ultimately,
burned out.
Now you play sad piano music
and I write melancholy poems
about a boy who,
in short,
loved me
once.

             You Lied When You Said I Wasn't Enough for You

You loved me,
but you didn't know how.
Because you loved me,
but you didn't know me.

How tragic it is, really.
You didn't get my
stories,
poems,
theories.
You wanted to cut
the very best parts.
The parts that hid -
me;
that would have let you know me.
And that's okay.
Fitzgerald said,
writers -
they are many people
all at once, and -
you loved one of me
and it was beautiful, but -
the rest of me?
They deserve love, too.
You loved me,
but you didn't know how.
Because you loved me, but -
you didn't know me -
you see?

I'm Not Very Good at Goodbyes, so How About a Fuck You?

I can sit here and pretend all I want that you ripped me to shreds,
I can pretend that you destroyed the essence of who I am,
pretend that my worth left when you did.
But that's all it would be; pretend
Because you hurt me, yeah;
you made me cry, made me want to hurt myself,
made me act on the latter, even,
but you didn't break me.
You say I'm too damaged and that I was naive.
I don't think I can be both and,
honestly, I don't think I was either.
I knew what I was getting myself into;
I'm destructive, darling, and that's something I just can't help.
Truth be told, I spent hours talking to my best friend
about how I knew you were going to hurt me,
how I knew there was no way this would last.
It was written all over you,
in every damn thing you said or did:
comments about my body,
or the future
or lack thereof
of your ex girlfriend.
And he got mad at me and sad for me,
desperately trying to get me to leave you,
but I didn't.
I didn't because I got addicted to the ways you hurt me:
the slight jabs about my looks,
implications that you would leave me,
eventually if not immediately,
hints that you weren't over her.
And what hurts the most
is that you post-marked all of these things with "I love you",
and you didn't.
Claim you did, whatever, that doesn't change anything,
because you didn't.
When you told me that you were falling for me,
you ended it, "with that being said, I don't know what love is."
And you still don't.
Because when you told me you loved me
it was with your breath pushing its way down my throat,
because you don't know love.
You know lust,
you know dependence,
you know possessiveness,
but you don't know love.
And that's what hurt.
And hurt it did,
but it did not break me.
I may be destructive,

but I would never give anybody the power to break me -
much less, you.

                    Faking Closure 101:
              An Unhealthy Guide in 4-5 Steps

Closure.
I'm beginning to think that this does not necessarily exist.
You can talk to your ex a million times,
burn the pictures,
hookup with another ex,
kiss his best friend,
and when it comes down to it,
you'll still be in love with him.
Or, maybe,
you'll just be hurt over what he did to you.
Or both.
You'll still come up with more questions you'd ask
if you thought you could stomach the answers -
you can't -
and then you'll come up with his answers
which will hurt
more or less
the same.

The first time we talked after we broke up,
he decided to be honest with me.
What a concept, right?
He told me that before we broke up,
he got together with his ex.
His pretty ex,
his skinny ex,
his artsy ex,
his quiet, sit down pretty, bite her tongue so as not to upset him,
ex.
And he told me he kissed her.
He said that, if it made me feel any better, I wasn't even on his
mind.
It didn't.

I decided that closure in the civil sense of it
just wasn't for me.
So I ripped out the journal pages about him.
You know,
all the lacy love poems and pretty polaroids;
the sugarcoated facade of something so much deeper than that.
And I burned them;
burned away the lies and the love and the loathing.

Tried to replace the love coiled deep within me with something uglier,
something deserving.
I just felt empty.

Burning things wasn't enough.
In something I've come to nickname
"prolonged masochism",
I still had all of my exes in my contact list.
Well, no, that's not quite right.
Only the exes who have hurt me.
And so I texted one;
not just any of them,
but specifically the one who only ever wanted sex.
Had a thing for stealing innocence, he said.
Turns out, he has a thing for girls who make bad choices when they're
sad, too.
If that's the case, I wonder why we broke up...
Anyways,
I just felt like I was lying to myself when all was said and done.
I'd say I felt used,
but that's nothing novel.

Maybe one of my exes wasn't enough.
Maybe I didn't want to heal,
maybe I wanted revenge.
So I found his friend who always hit on me, right?
You'll recall that too much of my identity is taken up by my ability
to make bad choices like it's nothing when I'm sad.
Or manic, or angry, or hurt, but that's besides the point.
I kissed him.
And then I felt dirty for doing so.
At least when he kissed his ex, it was because he still wanted her.
It was wrong, but genuine,
and maybe you can only ask for one or the other.
When I kissed his friend
it was like giving up my principles;
breathing them into some stranger's mouth,
giving away who I am via awkward stumbling around new terrain.
I didn't let it go any further.
That doesn't make a difference, does it?

And so finally, I began to fabricate dialogue.
Why don't you love me anymore?
I never did.
Why did you kiss her?

I never got over her.
What does your new girlfriend have that I don't?
Everything.
Why wasn't I enough for you?
Baby, do you really think you're enough for anyone?

To the Boy Who Broke My Heart and Ruined My Summer

I thought I was in love with you for a while,
I like to think I was wrong.
I don't hate you but I heavily resent you and wish you were never in
my life.
I know you think you didn't do anything wrong,
but on my end,
yikes,
I can't help but think you're awful.
And also I hope you other ex dislikes or,
let's be real,
hates you as much as I do.
And it's petty, I know,
but I hope everyone you love in your immediate future
breaks you like it's nothing.
And I hope you
break your favorite guitar like it's everything.
Because it is, isn't it?
It's all you've got,
kind of like how I convinced myself
you were all I had.
And good luck writing a breakup song called "Angie"
for your stupid album,
because that's totally not a rip off of my namesake.
I know you said some girls are not for falling in love with
but, rather,
good song writing material,
so I'm sorry that backfired.
But that's really on you, isn't it?
I'm a person, not a song
and you're a regret, not a person.

Sincerely,

A girl you used, because she's used to being used

Dramatic Irony

A boy I loved once told me
that some girls aren't for falling in love with;
some girls are just good song material.
I smiled and curled into him,
ignoring the misogyny,
thinking it was beautiful
in a sad sort of way.
I didn't realize he was talking about me.

It shouldn't have made a difference.

Off the Mark

I hate the summer.
It's too hot, you know?
Ice melting too fast,
mosquitoes humming too loud,
everything sticking together.
Sticking together like -
- us.
Entangled for weeks at a time,
walks on the beach,
soft, slow music,
stolen kisses beneath fireworks;
all the cliches,
beautiful and bright.
Beautiful and bright like -
- summer
Except not, you know?
Summer comes every year,
you only existed once.
And I always hated summer,
I used to love you.

Closure (for real this time)

It's your birthday.
I knew
before the notification.
17;
our relationship began.
18;
I am a memory.
It aches,
but it doesn't hurt.

The Truth Behind the Infamous Illusion

So, fuck, here we are.
Are you reading this?
You know I hate confrontation,
but I'm willing to try for the sake of -
well,
for the sake of myself,
if anything.
The yellow bird was an illusion,
but we were not.
I guess I have to accept that.
Isn't that what this section is leading up to?
I can't speak for you,
but I did love you.
I don't anymore.
I guess I have to accept that, too.
You were never my yellow bird,
but you were a damn good chameleon.
Slowly, though, your mask dissolved;
you hated my
friends
      mind
            sharp tongue.
You hated my body,
though you were the one to call me pretty
under the street lamps outside of kennedy park
the first time we met.
Ultimately, you hated the key parts of what made me, me.
You hated the things I lied about and the things I didn't think I had
to lie about.
But the past is the past.
So I guess you were a pseudo soulmate
while I was a trademark experiment.
Now we're strangers
forever under the false impression
that we still know each other in and out
(we never did).

Part 4: Miscellaneous Musings

You'll Thank Me Later

And it really is a goddamn shame
that we'll never break this shell;
I will not let you waste your time
just to see what it will tell.

So goodbye my chance
at happily ever after,
I wish we could dance,
just once more.

I cannot risk getting attached.

Some Nights, I Feel Nostalgic"

Last night,
I sat outside
with two girls
who are beginning to be
my best friends.
We got as high as the stars,
said "I love you"
in circles,
and found peace in each other
in ways we never could
in ourselves.

(None of us talk anymore.)

Hotels

Hotels feel more like home than my house ever has.
I don't know why.
Something about that predictability of departure,
you know?

gods

Humanity; communal fear of memories
that don't belong to us,
but our bodies.
We are not our flesh;
we are not physical beings.
We have no concept of pain,
but our bodies do,
and so we act as slaves to them,
allowing them to enlighten us
on the meaning of suffering.
Silly immortals,
we've forgotten the safe word.

                    That's Cool, but Just Hit on Me, Please.

Listen, I'm not pretty.
I have ugly, scraped up legs,
stretch marks from my constant change in eating habits,
fried hair and messy makeup,
practically translucent skin with imperfections everywhere.
My eyes expose me for who I am,
my mouth is always a little too accepting of kisses,
my nose too small and my eyebrows too pronounced.
I don't know how to fucking dress myself;
denim on denim, torn tights and shredded shirts.
My voice is too loud or too soft,
catching on words that mean anything.
I'm not pretty or soft or anything of romantic value;
I guess I've come to terms with that,
maybe you can just hit on me anyways.

About Another Poet

I don't know what I'm doing here.
I don't know if you know what you're doing, either.
(I hope you do)
But we were clearly supposed to meet.
Why?
I hope to find the answer in this poem.
(I won't)

About Seeing a Balloon Float Away

It's tragic, you know?
Every time I see a balloon floating away
I get sick to my stomach;
something darker than butterflies,
perhaps black widows or wasps.
I can't help but hear the child cry
as their beloved balloon slips from their fingers,
because their grip is not yet strong enough,
their mind not yet focused enough.
Can you imagine being that innocent?
Losing something that was temporary, anyway,
and immediately crying
as if it were the end of the world?
I guess I'm like that fictitious child.
In fact, I AM that fictitious child.
I was always the sensitive kid,
crying over lost balloons and dead field mice and misplaced toys;
I craved permanence, stability.
I'm still that sensitive child,
terrified of loss and death and things misplaced.
I cry over lost flings and dead feelings and misplaced worth;
I cry over everything, really;
things that aren't mine and things that will never be.
It's not my balloon,
but the empathy for that child swells within me.

Meanwhile, the vender selling the balloons shrugs off the loose
balloon;
he'll sell another.

For Erick

Rolling life, passing on,
never ending, until it does;
walks on the beach, turn to hospital stays,
and amiable smiles turn to dust.

Sometimes it gets better before getting worse,
contrary to the cliche;
happily-ever afters don't always win out,
submitting to disease and decay.

And the grandfather says to his grandson,
"Oh, hello, what are you doing here?
I'm happy to see you, don't get me wrong,
but I expected it to be years."

And he smiles a bittersweet smile,
because he's missed him for quite some time;
but in the scheme of things, he's still a child,
much too young for them to reunite.

Swan Song

I miss your lips;
nicotine,
wine,
laughter,
nostalgia,
parallel universe.

Ballad for a Love that Does Not Yet Exist, or Hasn't Existed for a
Long Time

Kiss me;
and by kiss me I mean
make the hectic world around us
seem dull in comparison
to our fabricated chaos.

Tell me I'm your salvation,
I'll tell you a lie of my own.
Maybe you're my deprivation,
maybe you just feel like home.

Cheap wine and a slant rhyme.
Swallow me whole, spit me out,
ask me to walk in a straight line.
Am I drunk on you or what you stole?
I guess it doesn't matter either way.

So let's fall in love at the end of the world,
maybe kill ourselves when it's said and done.
But for now, look into my eyes like it means something,
I know you know what it's like to be numb.

To the Boy on the Bus with the Sad Eyes and Pretentious Glasses

    I wanted to sit with you. Sit quietly and grab your hand. I
wanted to tell Candra I'd catch up with them so I could walk with and
look at art with you. I wanted to make a comment while we were
admiring the same piece and I wanted you to smile or respond or
something. I wanted to say something every time you looked in my
direction. I wanted to pretend you were the art and watch. I wanted to
smile wide but my timid nature got the best of me. I wanted a lot of
things, but I ignored myself. I wonder if I'll forget you by next
month.

Sincerely,
    A momentary admirer

Inspiration, Personified

Tattered minds think alike,
isn't that the old saying?
Or maybe I've got some of it skewed.
Shattered hearts beat together,
or something like that,
do you think you believe that's true?

I don't know either,
if that makes you feel better,
but I'm willing to buy into the hype.
I don't know what I'm doing,
if it's all the same to you,
but perhaps you're becoming my type.

So we'll write some more poetry,
bounce ideas off each other,
never sure if we'll wake up tomorrow.
We'll pick our way through the ruins
and document the nights,
forgetting all we've ever borrowed.

                    Sunkissed Salvation

Fate;
I didn't used to believe in it.
It was some fictitious, romanticized thing,
like unicorns, or love.
But something about this summer,
something about these first few days,
with looming clouds
and evening coffee
and an endless flow of poetry,
feels a lot like something more.
Last summer,
all of my arguments against love vanished.
Though love hurts,
I can't say love doesn't exist,
because I felt it in the core of my soul,
held my love's hands in my own,
experienced what it's like to have it taken away.
So I have yet to see a unicorn,
but last summer,
all of my arguments against love vanished.
This summer,
I feel myself giving way to fate,
feel my guard dropping and my reservations slipping away.
I don't know why.
I don't know if it's necessarily a good or bad thing.
But it sure has given me something to write about.

                    Tell Me

How I make you feel,
what my eyes remind you of,
what you think of when you think of me
(if you think of me),
why you talk to me,
who you are,
your biggest fear,
your greatest desire,
if you want to kiss me,
anything,
everything,
a secret.

Things Change

I thought we were soulmates.
I don't know if I miss you.

After Reading <u>The Secret History</u> by Donna Tartt

Maybe part of me is desperate to study under that cold-hearted
professor.
Maybe part of me is obsessed with
all-consuming friendships,
beautifully toxic relationships,
and dangerous secrets.
Maybe it's all I really know,
and maybe I just want it on a bigger scale.
I want danger -
the intense kind,
the kind that people write stories about;
not the kind that just leaves me fucked in the head.
Maybe I'm sick of small scale destruction;
maybe I want to watch the world go up in flames.

A Series of Small Details that Remain in My Life, Subtly Reminding Me
of What I Had with You

Your nickname in my phone;
we don't talk anymore, so I don't see it like I used to,
but it crosses my screen from time to time,
reminding me of what could have been, or what was,
or whatever the story is -
we never did clarify.

The scar on my shoulder;
when I think back upon exes and scars,
the memories are just short of catastrophic
but we were never anything official.
And so I guess it makes sense that the scar I got from you
is the only scar I have
with a story of whimsy rather than woe.
Would it make sense to you if I told you that hurt worse?
I know it would.

2 a.m.;
I've stayed up until this time with my fair share of people,
but something about you made it different.
There was never one specific topic, you know?
We dabbled in mismatched philosophy and tragic backstories,
outlandish sarcasm and shameless flirtation.
I wouldn't say it was innocent
but it was comfortable and,
honestly,
I think that's what matters to me the most.
Would you believe me if I told you I'd never felt comfortable like
that with somebody before?
Of course you would,
you've heard the stories

Butterflies;
an endless cliche,
passed down from generation to generation.
And I know we spent a lot of time making fun of cliches,
mostly because we *are* cliches,
but I told a friend
after you kissed me the first time,
that the butterflies were more intense
than any I've ever felt before.
I said that you tasted like magic.

I asked myself if I believed in magic –
do you?
I think I stopped when you found it with someone else.
It's interesting how the beginning of something great can remain that
for eternity –
an isolated beginning.

Cliffhangers;
because that's what we are, more or less.
We're the cliffhanger at the end of a chapter
of a book the author abandoned.
We're an almost, a maybe, a what if
and that's all we can be, I guess.
There's a theory that there is a window of opportunity
and if you don't take advantage, the opportunity could be lost
forever.
You had to take that chance with her,
and I get that,
but I've been the second choice of so many
and I don't think I can be that for you.

So if the magic runs out and
you find yourself missing the way my fingers brushed against your
collarbones,
or the way we always seemed to be awake at the same time,
or our shared sense of humor,
please, by all means, write about me.
Or, Play the drums, because that's your thing.
Watch a marvel movie,
drink a cup of coffee,
listen to "I MIss You" –
but please don't come back.

Because, yeah,
I miss you and the magic.
And, yeah,
I want the rest of the book.
But I don't think I can handle being your second choice
after everything you made me feel,
because you were different and, frankly, I want to keep it that way.
So, stay in my past.
Stay that whirlwind romance that amounted to nothing
but a few fading hickeys and a handful of inside jokes.
Stay an almost because an almost isn't rejection;
an almost is fate changing its mind.

But a second choice, a second choice is you letting me know that you
want me,
but not enough,
and that's far too familiar.
And magic should always have an air of mystery.

Evolution of an Egotist

I crave change,
expressed
through my hair;
bleached
     because I can't sleep.
Purple
     because he said
          blondes are his type.

I can't be a type;
          I am
             ever-changing.

Bleached Skin

I've found it easy to throw away the pictures,
and easier yet to hack away the pain
(temporarily).
But when it comes down to it,
it's too easy.
When it comes down to it,
that's not where the memories lie.
You'll find yourself throwing away armfuls of clothing;
clothing they touched you in,
clothing they merely saw you in.
And, even then, you'll feel them on your skin.

Contradictions

You were my lifeline
and now you're dead.
If you're in heaven now,
where the hell does that leave me?

Photographic Visionary

My best friend
looks at the
cityscape
like it's her
whole world.
She's leaving it behind
in August.
There are bigger things.

                        You Suggested It,
              but I'm Going to Write a Poem About It

Let's change it up a bit.
We can listen to artificial rain
and I'll curl up on your floor
in a cocoon of blankets.
You'll stay up and write poetry
about whatever's on your mind in that moment.
Maybe, I won't wake up from a nightmare,
crying and shaking.
Maybe, I'll sleep peacefully,
knowing somebody has taken my place,
at least for the moment.
Maybe I can't sleep because I have too much to say;
maybe I won't sleep because I'm afraid of what will happen if I do.
Maybe it *is* just simply insomnia;
maybe it's complexly self-inflicted.

                         Warm Milk

So, fuck it, let's do it;
let's take cheap trains to Seattle.
Let's eat gas station food,
and take blurry pictures,
and scribble down poetry.
Let's make each other laugh,
and talk about everything,
and love every stranger we meet.
I'll get a tacky tattoo of the space needle,
you'll hold my hand while they do it.
We'll look at apartments
that we'll each live in one day.
I'll drink lots of coffee,
while you eat dark chocolate,
and we'll get lost in the soul of the city.
We'll drink shitty vodka
and smoke til our lungs hurt
all to be pained and perfect poets.
So, yeah;
fuck it, let's do it.

I'm in Someone Else's Dream

Crushed ice and diet soda,
eyelash wishes and menthol cigarettes.
The silhouette girls sit on the pavement,
basking in moonlight and laughter
as they look at the stars.
If you really focus,
you can feel the earth stop in its orbit
to breathe in their unconditional and uncorrupted love.

Lukewarm coffee and untouched breakfast,
frayed book pages and hard candy.
The shadows sit silently at the table
as the sun washes the walls golden.
Their eyes wander around the room,
desperate to settle but no longer on each other.
They used to be in love,
but that was lifetimes ago.
Now, they are nothing more than exhausted,
and together they write a symphony of deep quiet.

A spirit rises as the dusk settles in
and tries to find her way back home.
She won't find her way and she knows it.
They all do;
the trees and the stars and kindred spirits.
Still,
They can't help but feel her hope for themselves.
The dead don't sleep, but they dream.
And what is a dream?
Maybe "dreaming" is just another way to say "going home."
And so the world breathes in and watches the spirit rise,
and she begins to head back home.

Overthinking Over Coffee

Born to be mute and mutilated,
raised to be all
toxic smoke and shattered mirrors.
I would like to just live in the moment,
but the fates have never been so forgiving.
Up with a familiar soul that knows me -
4 a.m. is a good feeling,
but they look to me and say,
"I don't know if I believe in tradition,
but when I get sad I talk to the sky
and call her God."
Sometimes I breathe in the galaxy
and could swear god is me.
I think my edges are too sharp, serrated.
I say shattered but I mean shattering;
prick your finger like sleeping beauty.
That is to say,
kiss danger,
and set yourself free.

Unholy Love

A kiss that knocked me dead
and an innocent grin to offset the poison.
All red lipstick and filterless cigarettes,
fangs like Dracula and a taste like coffee and fog.
You touched me once and pulled me in,
hands like a vice grip and voice like hypnosis.
Seductive sedative playing dress up,
all feathered wings and glowing halo;
I prayed to a god I never believed in and got you instead.
You, all counteractive salvation
and lips prepared for prayer;
body like a hallowed church,
all intricate detail and overflowing garden.
I was a disciple and you,
oh, you were the teacher so drunk on narcissism,
you claimed savior and I believed you.
One day I came looking for you,
only to find the empty ruins of something unrecognizable.
Nothing but a wisp of smoke hung in the air
to prove to me that you existed.

Damaged Goods

We've been drinking and I know you want to kiss me.
Not because I'm pretty or because you like me,
but because you're intoxicated,
and you crave closeness.
You know me better than everyone,
which means you know too much,
but obvious character flaws don't tend to matter
once you get past midnight.
You're probably thinking about how I would react,
or your heartbreak and how it still feels fresh
even though it was a year and a half ago,
or maybe you're not thinking about anything at all.
Your hand is on my thigh and I didn't notice,
or maybe you just put it there,
but I guess that doesn't matter.
I think I would kiss you back,
but I wouldn't initiate it
because I love you
and I hate myself
and that probably doesn't mean what you think it does.
But, again, who am I to say what you're thinking or not thinking?
I've been hurt by more people who've kissed me than haven't.
I'm bipolar and maybe that makes it easy
to both love and hate me.
I joke about trauma so much,
that I remain convinced I don't care
until something stupid sets me off.
Once,
the one who hurt me most bit my lip so hard,
I swear my mouth flooded salty red
and drowned me dead.
Another time,
I think he tried to kill me.
But I'm here with you,
and you want to kiss me,
because you're drunk
and scared that you might end up alone.
So, yeah, you can kiss me,
but all you'll taste is expired blood.

Part 5: Revelations

In Which My, 'I Want to be Happy' Playlist is Composed of My Favorite
Sad Songs . . .

I don't know what's wrong with me. I want to get better, somewhere
deep down. But what if I've lost the motivation to want to be okay? I
think I've given up. Not consciously, but so slow that it's just now
catching up with me. The Social Animals aren't a happy band and all of
their songs are on here. It's like i just can't resonate with happy. I
must have been happy at some point. I don't think I would have
survived otherwise. So why can't I remember? It's like the fog on
campus is inside of my skull. Nothing feels right. My phone won't
charge and I'm not tying too hard to fix that. I just don't want to
talk to anyone, but I hate being alone. It's hard, you know. I don't
think I've given myself any time for reflection and evaluation. I
don't even know what I want out of life, I just say I do because I
want someone to be proud of me. I'm allegedly not a fuck-up, but is
that just because no one really knows me? I don't even know who I am.
I know who I'm being and who I should and who I used to be but I don't
know who I really am and what I want and what I should do. What are my
goals? My ambitions? I really just want to drink good coffee and pick
flowers and write and read and go on adventures. Truthfully, I am lost
- and have an essay to write.

A Few Small Guesses

Maybe I'm searching for salvation.
Maybe I always have been.
I don't really know what that means;
more than that,
I don't know where to find it.
Kiss me hard,
      show me you want me,
hold my hand in the rain,
      tell me something I'd never guess.
Maybe I'm not searching for salvation.
Maybe I'm yearning for
love
      connection
                  passion.
Maybe these are the components of salvation.
This is just a guess.

About Falling in Love with a Stranger

This is going to sound stupid,
but I love, love.
I love
hearts beating in sync,
fingertips brushing against each other,
cloudy thoughts and clarity -
somehow simultaneously;
consume me.

Floral Fixation

I started keeping plants in my room
sometime during my 15th year.
The idea was that
if I had something other than myself to sustain
I would keep going.
I would get out of bed,
I would stay alive
to make sure my plants stayed alive.
At first, this seemed to work.
Until my plants started dying
no matter what I tried.
I couldn't even control myself,
so what did I expect?
If I couldn't keep them alive,
what was I doing here?

Everything

I've been burning dead flowers.
I wanted to destroy something,
something more fragile than I,
and I wanted to reduce this something
to something else;
something powder light and smoke heavy.
I wanted to make art with the reduced something.
I wanted to get my hands temporarily dirty
and make something tragically beautiful
and half reminiscent
of the original dead flower.

No, that's not right.
The dead flower was alive, once;
beautiful and delicate still, yes,
but alive.
That had never occurred to me.

Another Unnecessary Poem About a Lost Love that Did or Didn't Matter

Things felt safe in your basement the way that they never seem to in
the real world.
I don't miss you, necessarily,
and if we're being honest, none of your friends really stood out to
me, either.
It was the environment, I guess;
the sense of togetherness.
"I got your back, no questions asked"
and friend holidays that always felt more authentic
than the calendar.
I got you guys into my favorite shitty music
and there was always coffee brewing when I woke up,
no matter what time.
We could stay there when you were at work,
and your mom always complimented my tights.
I don't know if there's a point to me writing this,
but I started college this fall and,
I don't know,
I've been wondering if there's much of a point to anything I write
these days.
I miss the easy.
Not that life was ever easy;
not for me, anyways.
Not for us.
Maybe I do miss you,
and maybe I know it wasn't meant to be,
and maybe that scares me.
Things aren't meant to be
most of the time.
I've known it forever and lately I don't like it;
it doesn't feel poetic anymore.
Just empty and sad.
Remember the night before you started working at Marc's
and she showed up with the dog?
She was crazy in our eyes,
in your eyes, really,
but we indulged her.
Is that what it was?
Did we all just indulge each other's musings and fantasies?
Dreams of road trips and being published,
shitty tours and night jobs?
Maybe we were in love with the ways we fell apart
and hastily pieced each other back together.

Does that make it any less authentic?
I was 17 and you were 19,
now I'm 18 and you're 20.
What's the difference?
You guys didn't know any better than I did
and I'll be damned if we know any better now.
What have you learned in the past 10 months?
I just have more questions.
You didn't have many questions at the time, and I think I admired
that.
Like Iggy, you had a lust for life,
and I just wanted everything to stop.
But for a few weeks, I was content.
Walking around with you guys at 3 a.m. that one time,
ending up at that goddamn church and laughing at the irony.
Recently I turned back to handfuls of neurontin.
Remember when I came over and he was fucked up
and watched Always Sunny and rambled away chaotically?
Or when the other thought her cheesy potatoes
were her pumpkin pie and smothered them in whipped cream?
I don't know what this is about anymore.
Longing or finality,
history or presence.
I guess in a few years I'll read this again and figure it out.
Maybe not.
Maybe I don't want to.
Truth be told, if I figure these things out,
I'll run out of things to write about.
I won't be the girl you fell in love with.
I don't aspire to be someone to fall in love with,
you know that;
I guess that factored into our brief magnetism.
But I do aspire to be the version of me I was when I was with you .
The problem is,
that wasn't me,
not really.
That was the reflection of you guys on me.
I want it,
god, I want it,
but I'm doomed to this:
unanswered questions and a nonspecific feeling.

Stop Searching for Metaphors at 1 a.m.

I put dead flowers in an old pill bottle.
They were too heavy,
so I watched the poor bottle stumble over.
Ironic.
Flowers are known to be frail,
and the dead are said to be powerless.
I guess anyone can make you fall
over yourself
and never get back up.

Things that Make Me Happy

~ good coffee ~ pretty plants ~ The Secret History by Donna
Tartt ~ music ~ the stars ~ writing ~ poetry ~ walks with
friends ~ cozy sweaters ~ doing my makeup ~ long naps ~
vintage clothing ~ thrift stores ~ singing and dancing
obnoxiously ~ bookstores ~ my skin care routine ~ change ~
chai lattes ~ my vinyl collection ~ lipstick ~ cats ~ art
museums ~ concerts ~ watching movies with mom ~ the week I
spent with my aunt ~ organization ~ the rain ~ feeling
loved and being right ~ tattoos ~ parks ~ banana pancakes ~
meeting new people ~ feeling better after crying ~ ink on
paper ~ bats ~ high waisted jeans ~ autumn & spring ~
studio apartments ~ halloween ~ playlists ~ Criminal Minds
~ candid photos ~ talking to my brother ~ movie theater
with my sister ~ ice cream ~ sunrises & sunsets ~ bodies of
water ~ philosophical discussions ~ weekends ~ long showers
~ the smell of cinnamon ~ driving around with friends ~
punk rock

Ashes to Ashes

I'm lying here in the grass,
ashes falling on me and mosquitos
drink my blood without permission.
The stars are faint with light pollution
and I am faint with distant daydreams.
My heart aches the same way
an astral body must when its light dies out.
Nobody notices it die until thousands of years too late,
and nobody noticed it was on its way out, ever.
Galaxy goddess turned burn out
never quite learned how to fly and
you decided it was time to orbit
Or maybe it was time for me to die,
so
now that I'm done breathing you in,
the way all of earth takes oxygen,
I inhale nothing more than the smoke trailing a comet.
I realize now that there's no difference
between you and toxicity,
so this poem is nothing more
than a tired tirade of space girl metaphors.

You Know How Sometimes You Get This Feeling Like You Miss Someone but
You Have No Idea Who?

Yes.
Kind of.
Maybe?
I think so.
That's the thing about feelings -
you never really can place what they are.
You can get a good idea,
paint it pretty
and give it a generic name:
love, happiness, sadness, anger,
but that's about it.
They say there's a compound German word
for practically any complex emotion
one might feel,
but I don't buy it.
If so,
show me the word for,
"I just realized I'm in love with my best friend, it's 4 a.m., my
sugar high is crashing,
I've got a caffeine headache,
and I've always been a tiny bit
scared of the truth, and love,
and, honestly, small dogs, while we're on
the subject of fear."
Or,
"I just remembered that everyone who's ever kissed me never loved me,
and I got anxious about it so now my arm hurts from the scratches and
also I don't know if I'm sad or relieved that my dad refuses to talk
to me."
See, German can try all it wants,
but people are too complex for
language to ever capture.
I guess that sort of makes this poem pointless.